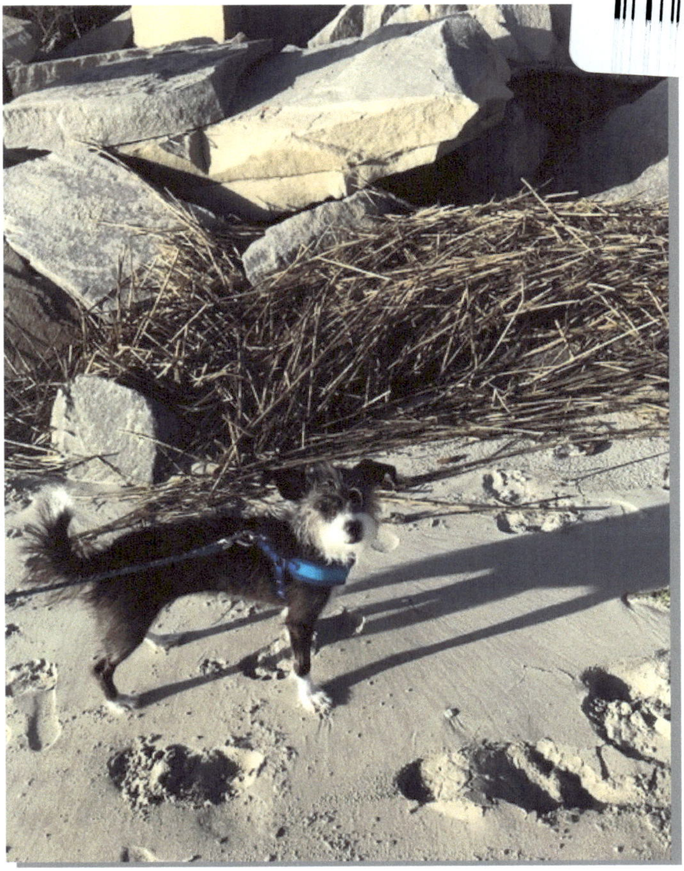

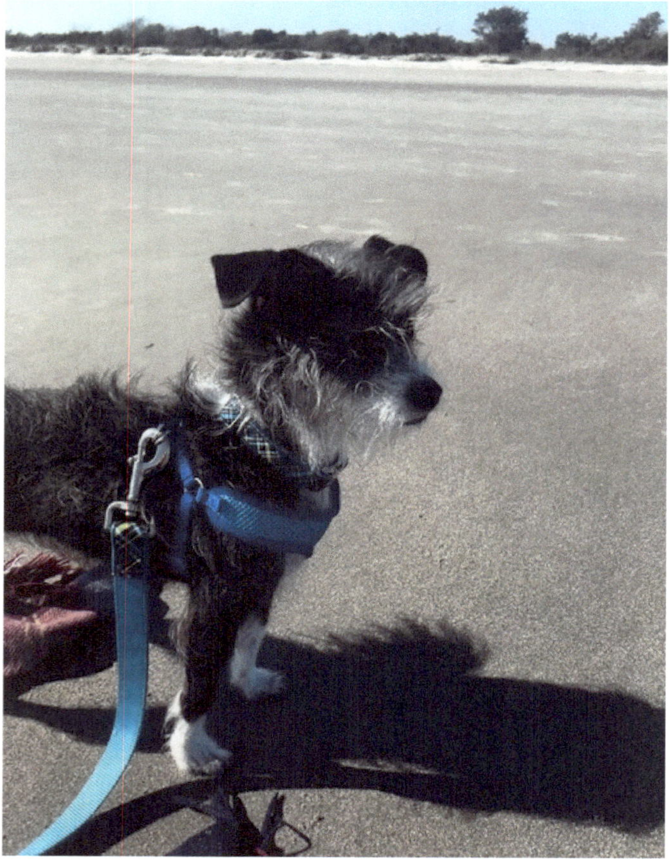

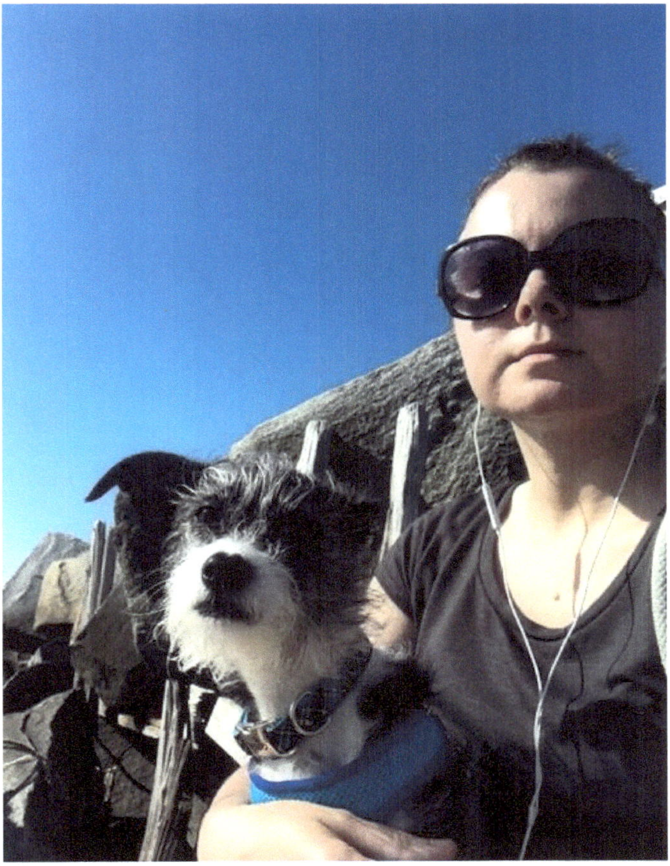

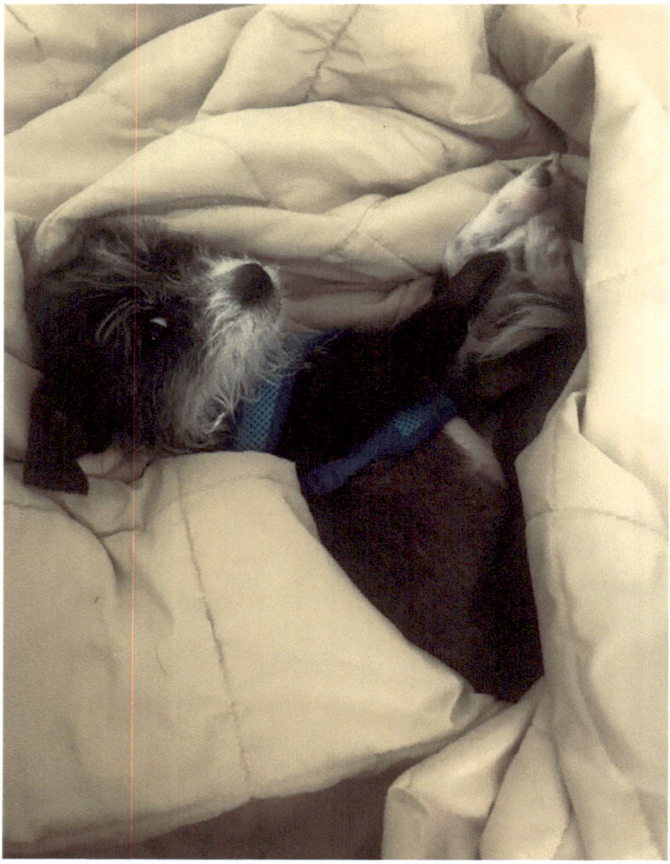

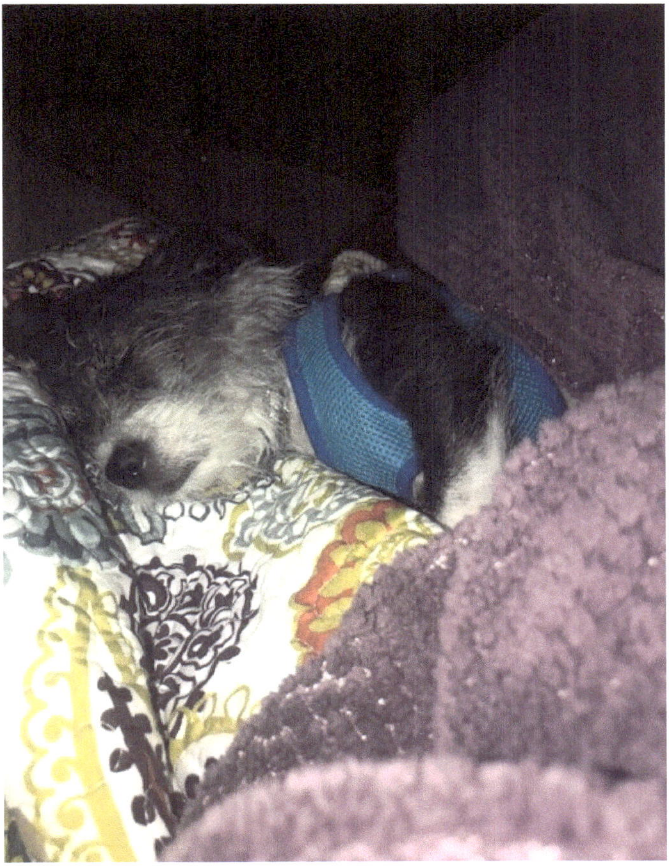

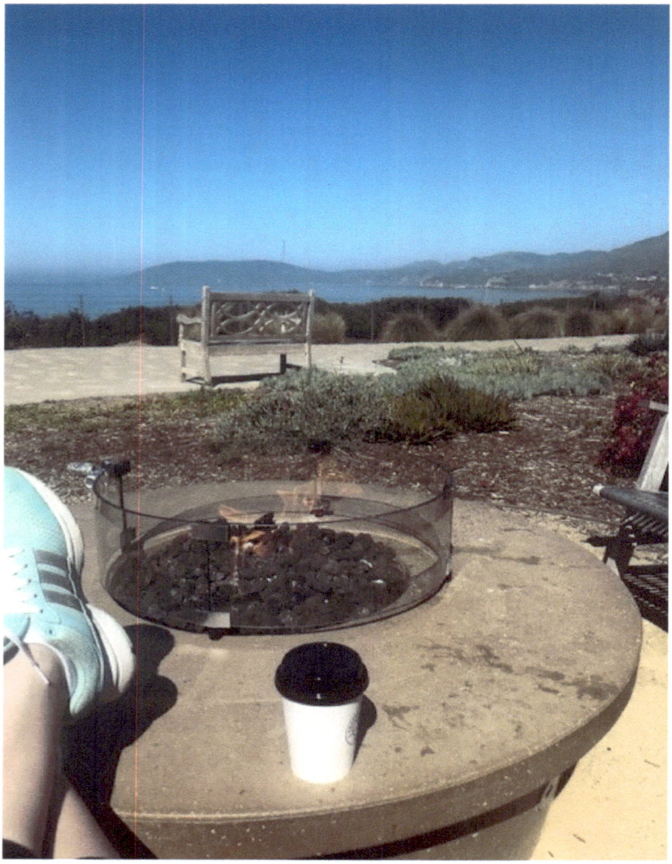

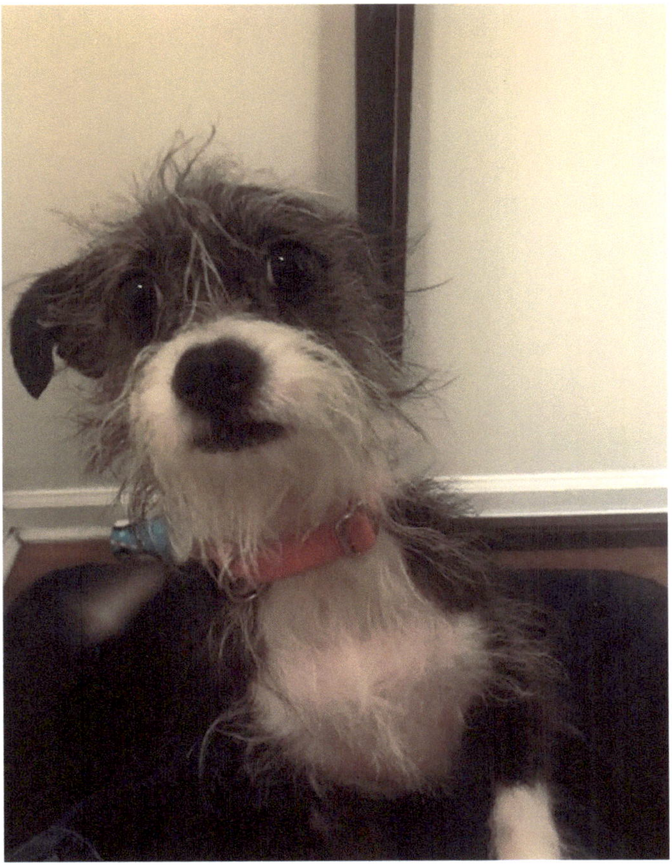

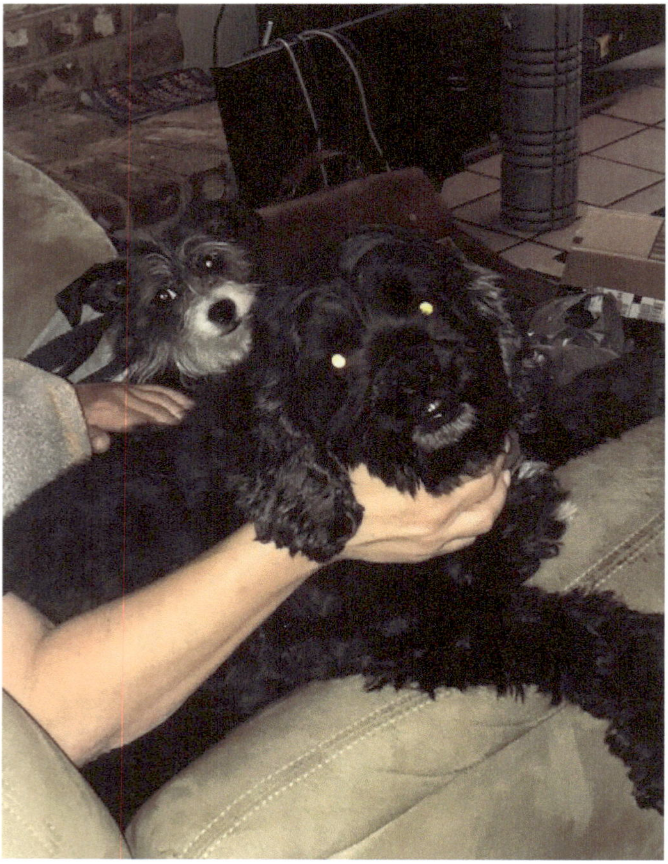

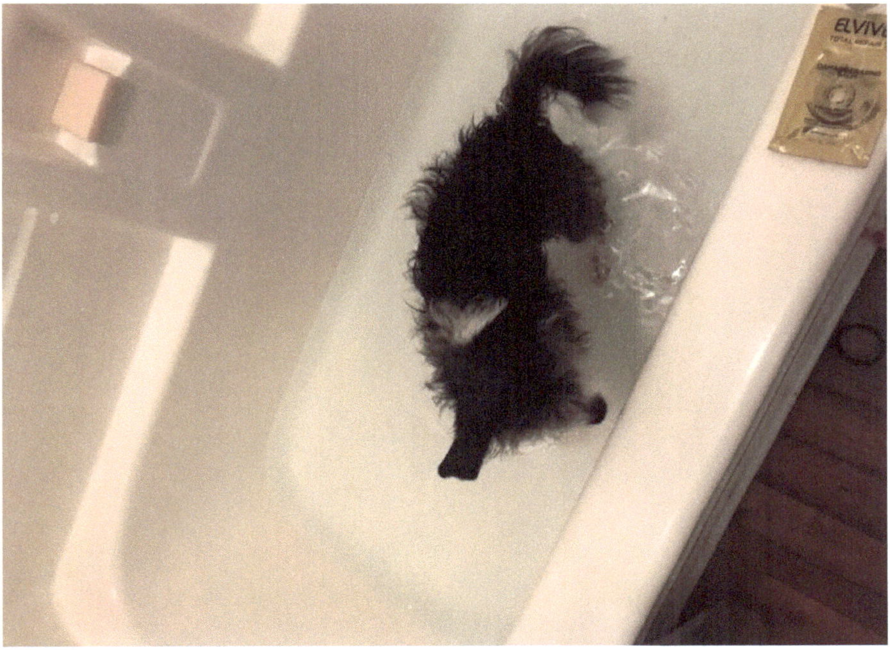

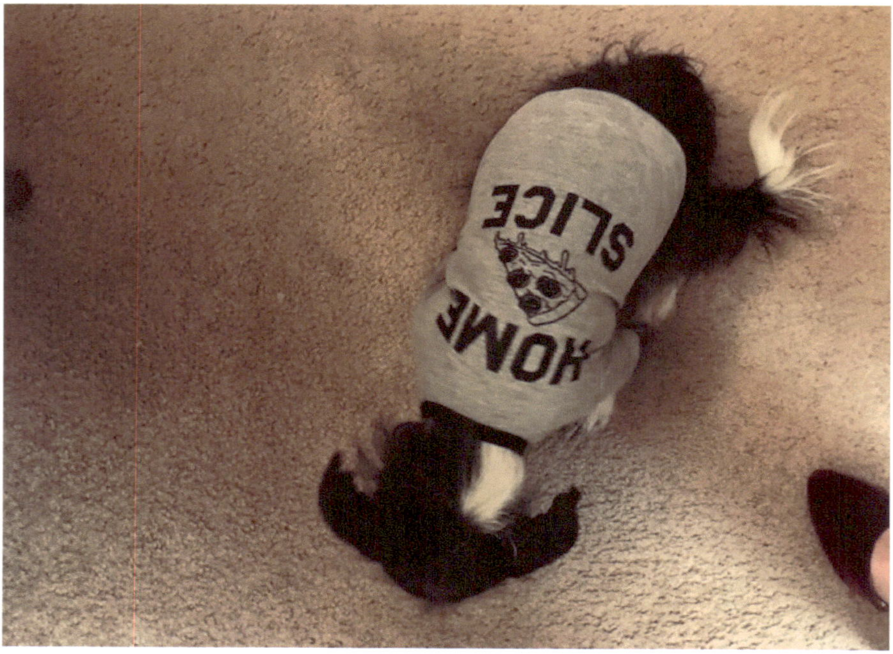
HOME
SLICE

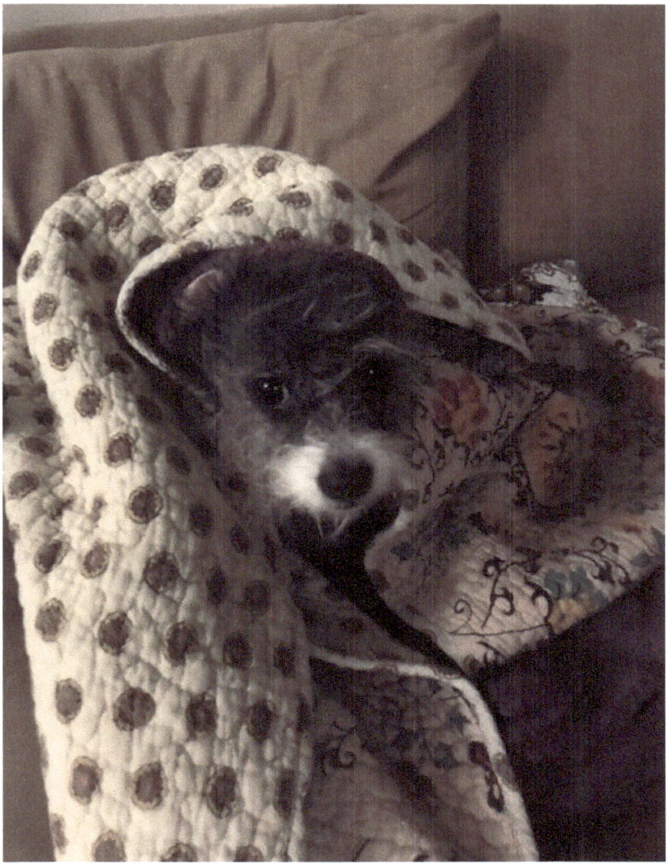

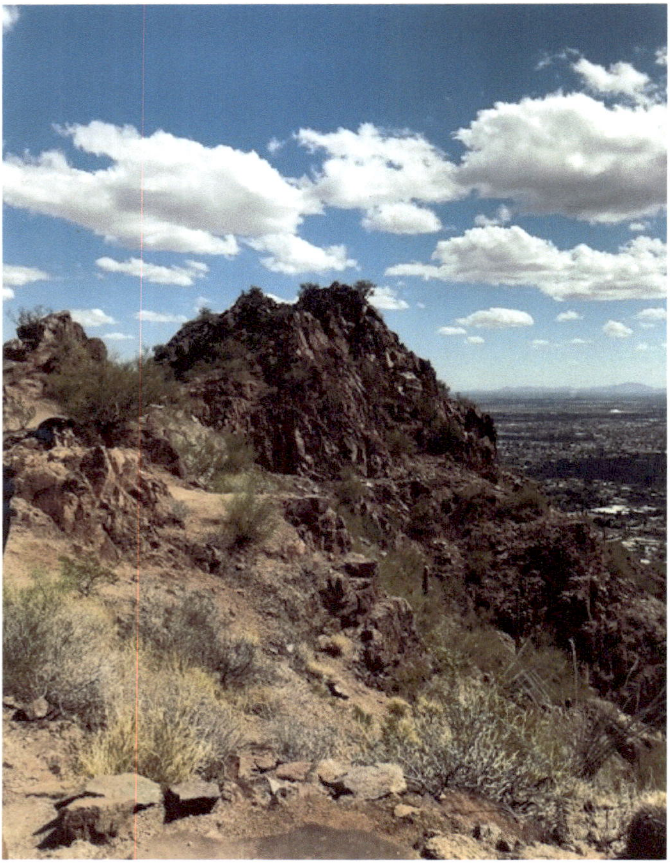

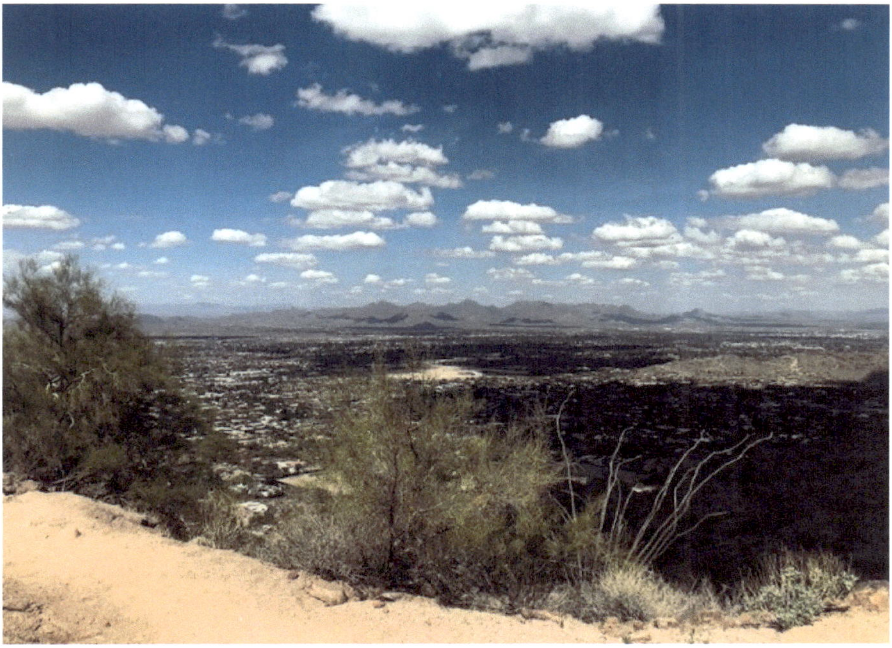

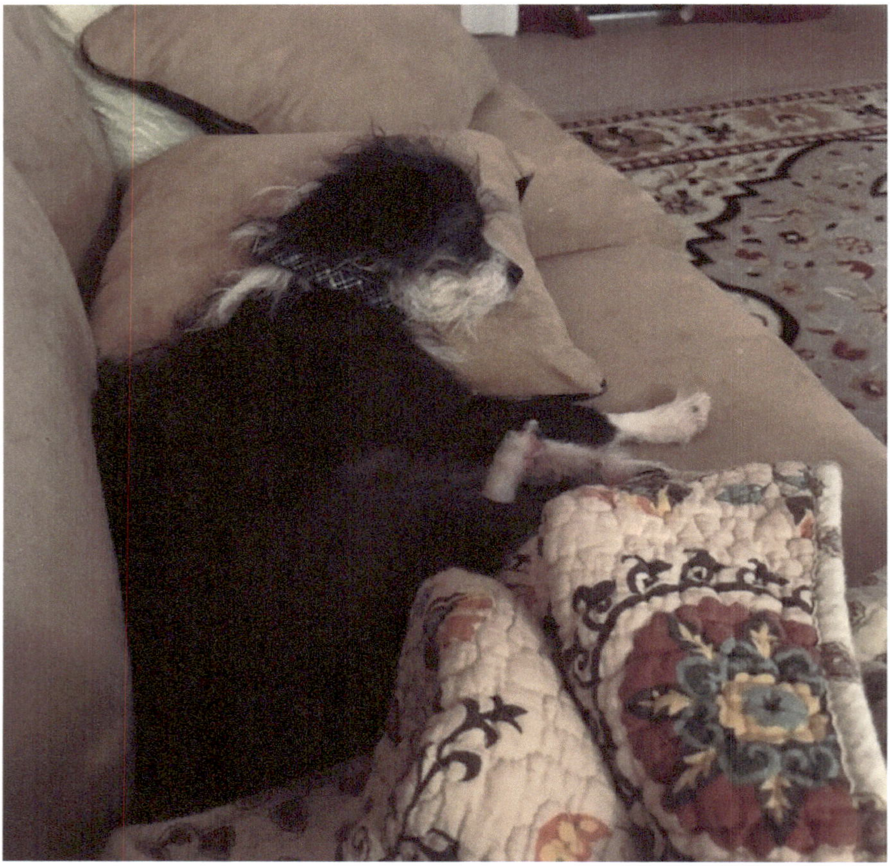

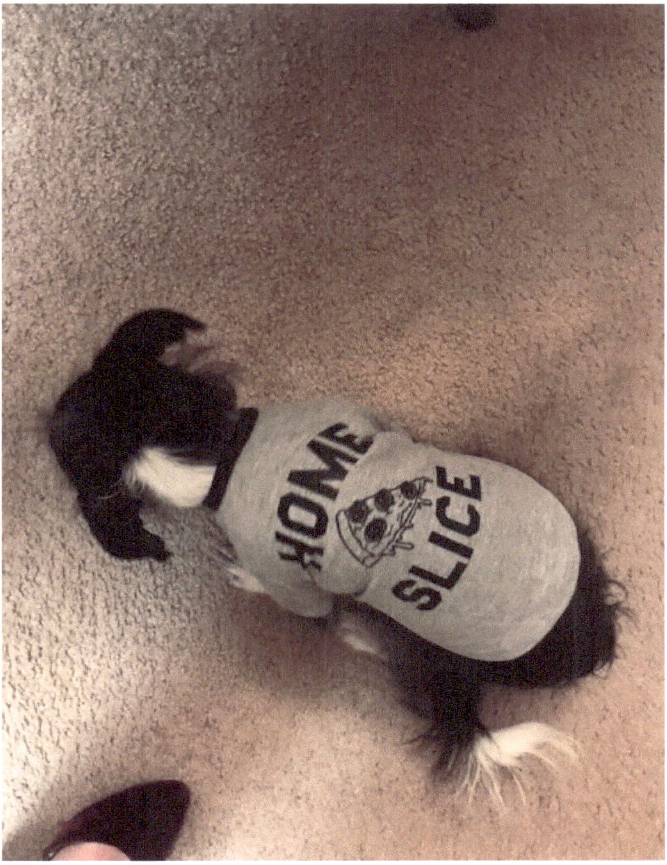
HOME
SLICE

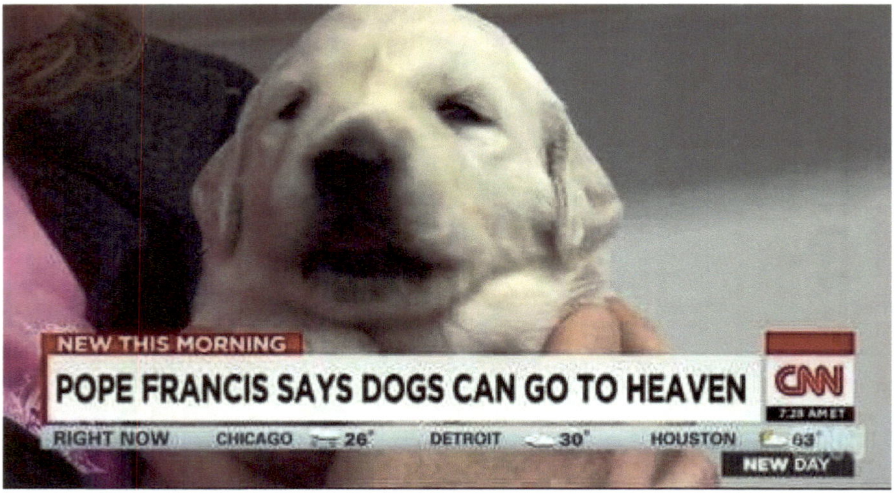
NEW THIS MORNING
POPE FRANCIS SAYS DOGS CAN GO TO HEAVEN
CNN
RIGHT NOW
CHICAGO 26°
DETROIT 30°
HOUSTON 63°
NEW DAY

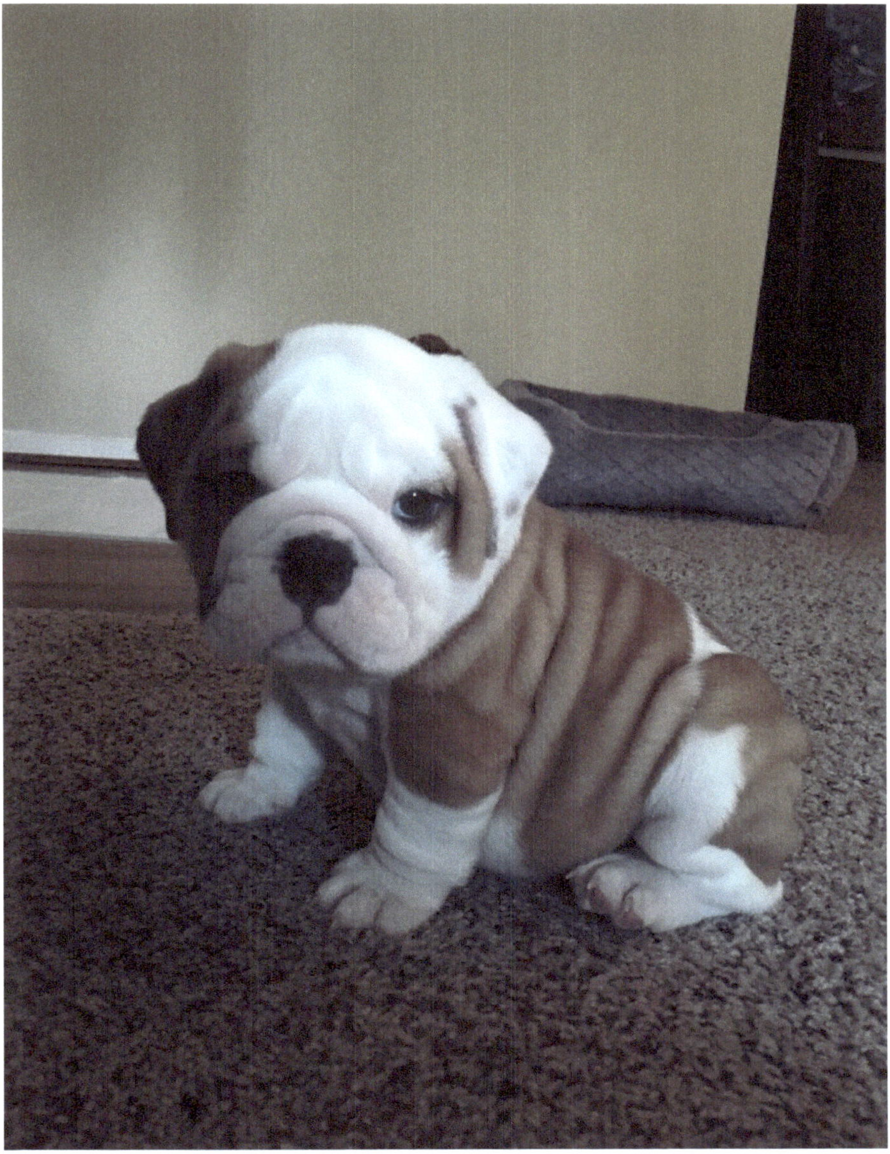

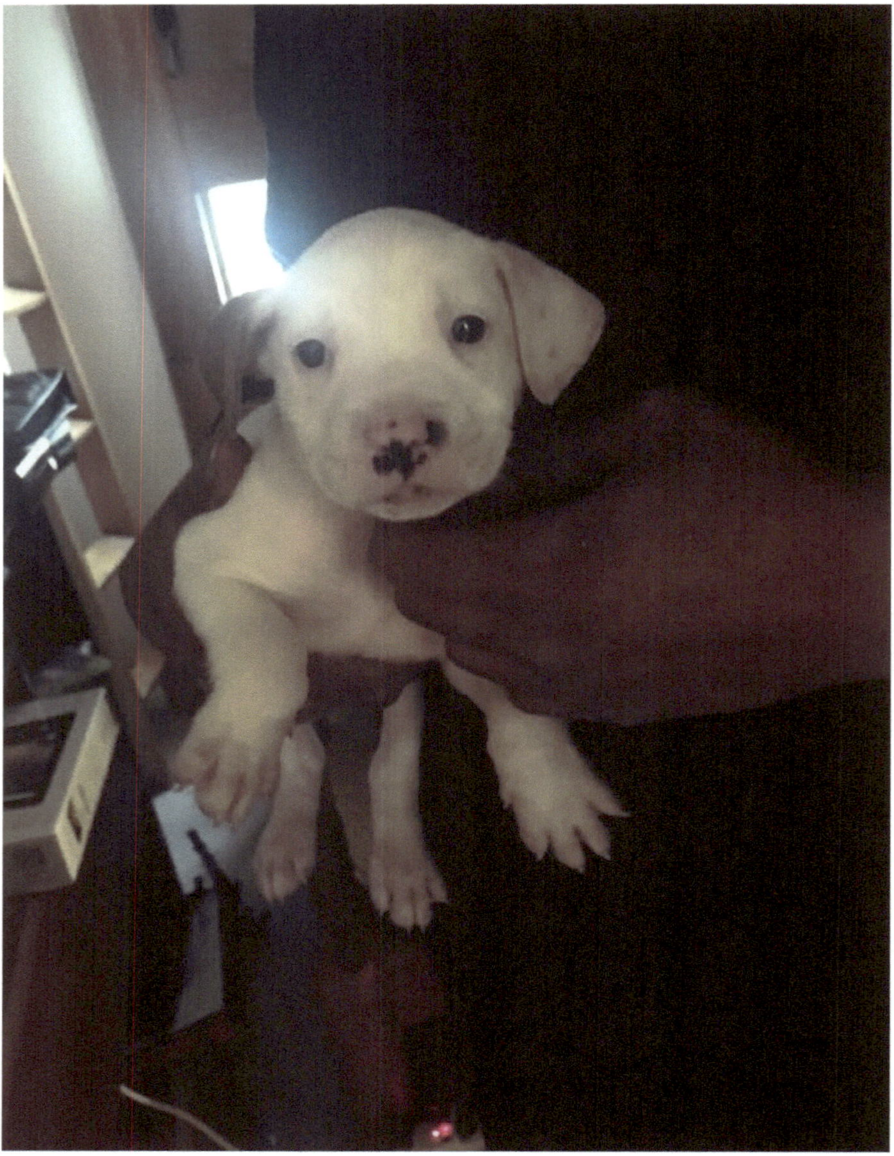

There's no such thing as a perfect nigh-

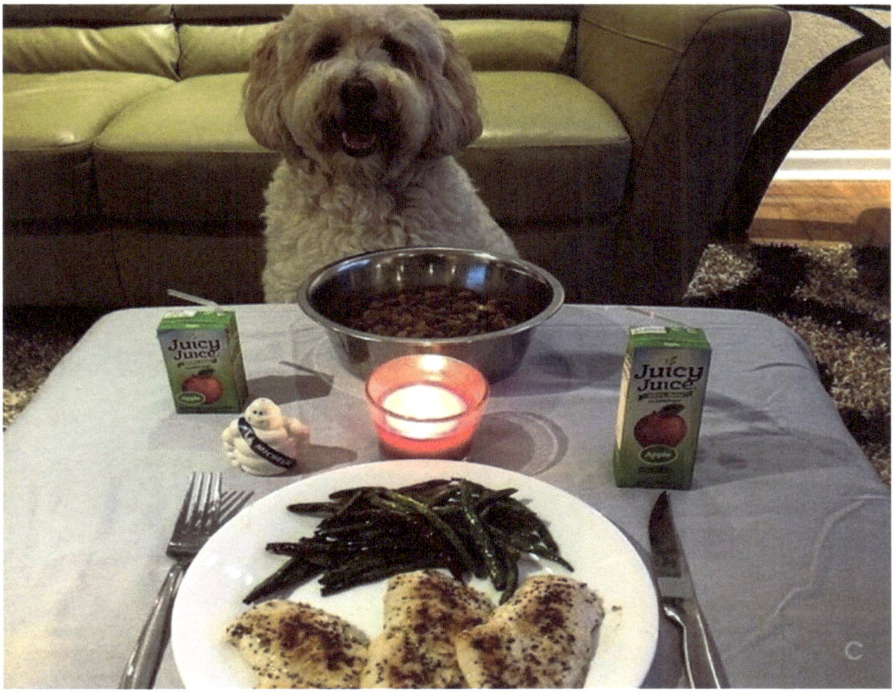

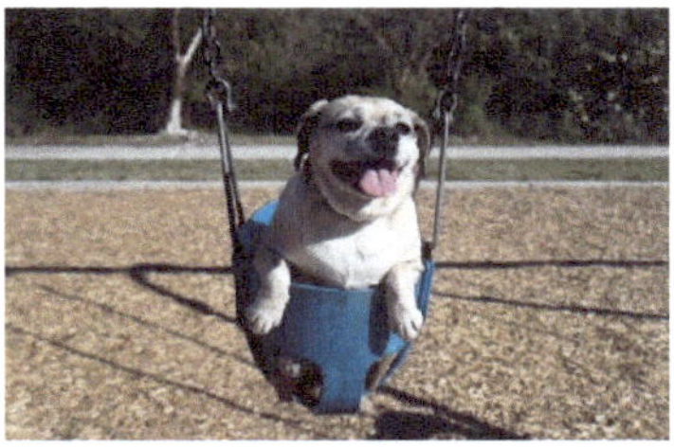

MY PARENTS ARE AT DISNEYLAND AND JUST SENT ME THIS

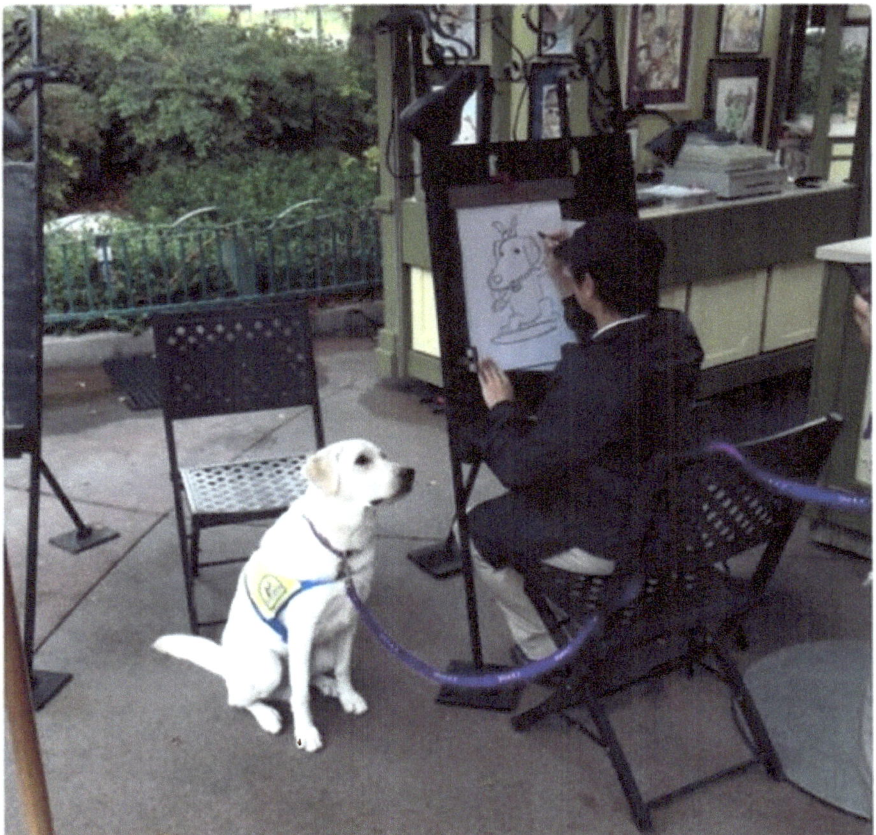

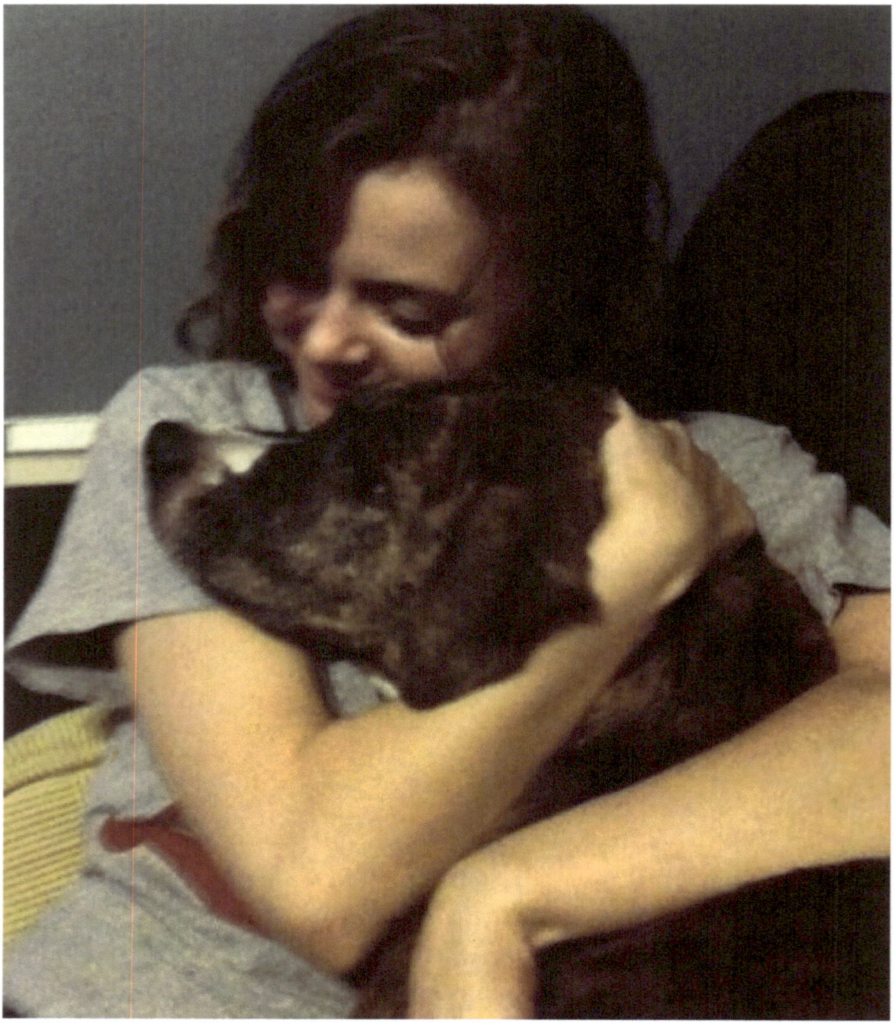

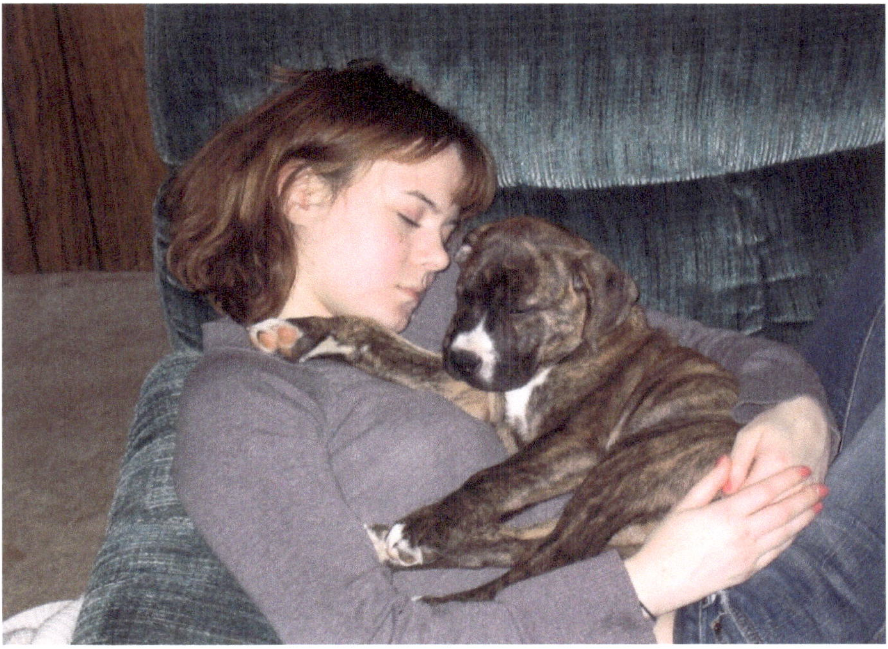

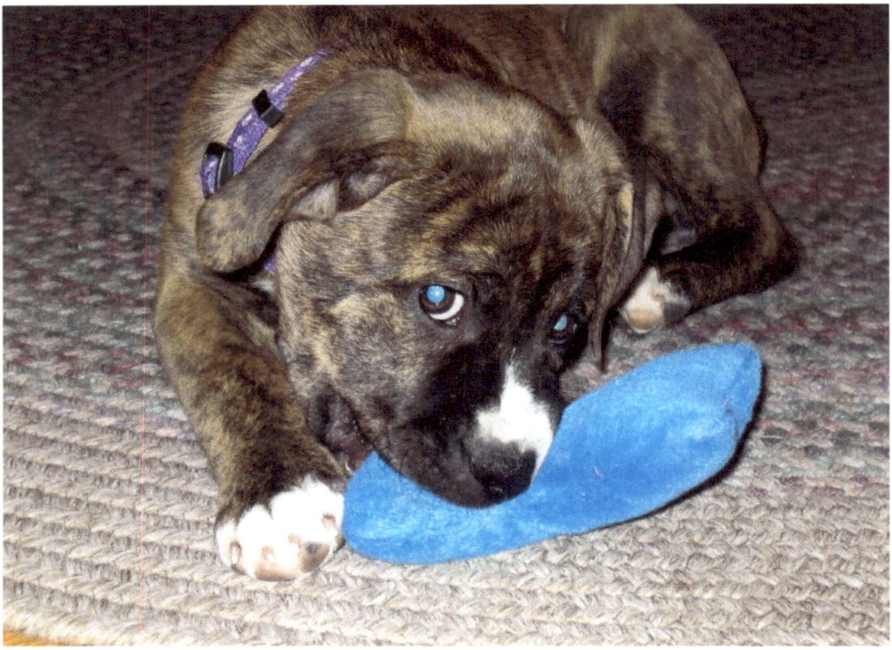

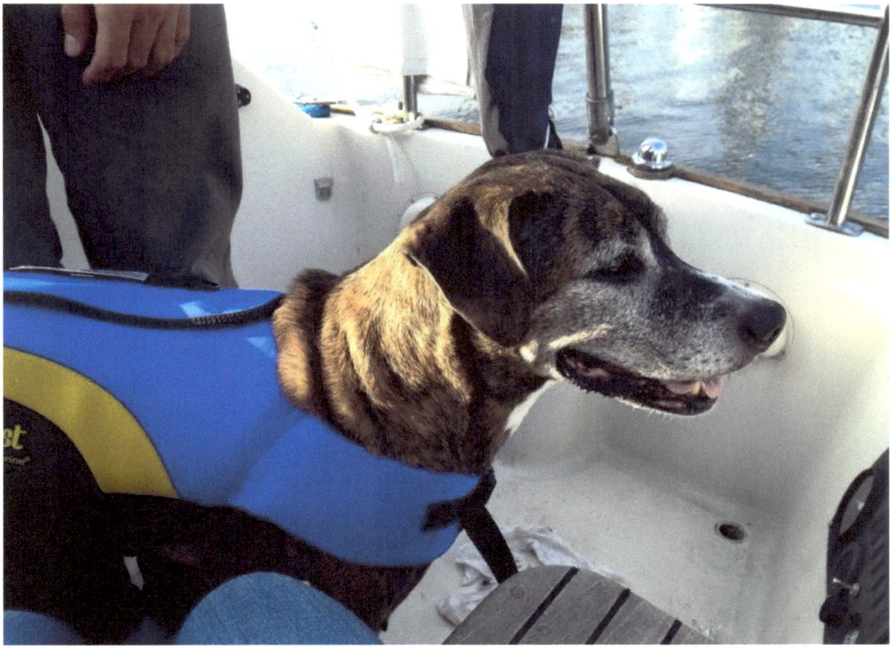

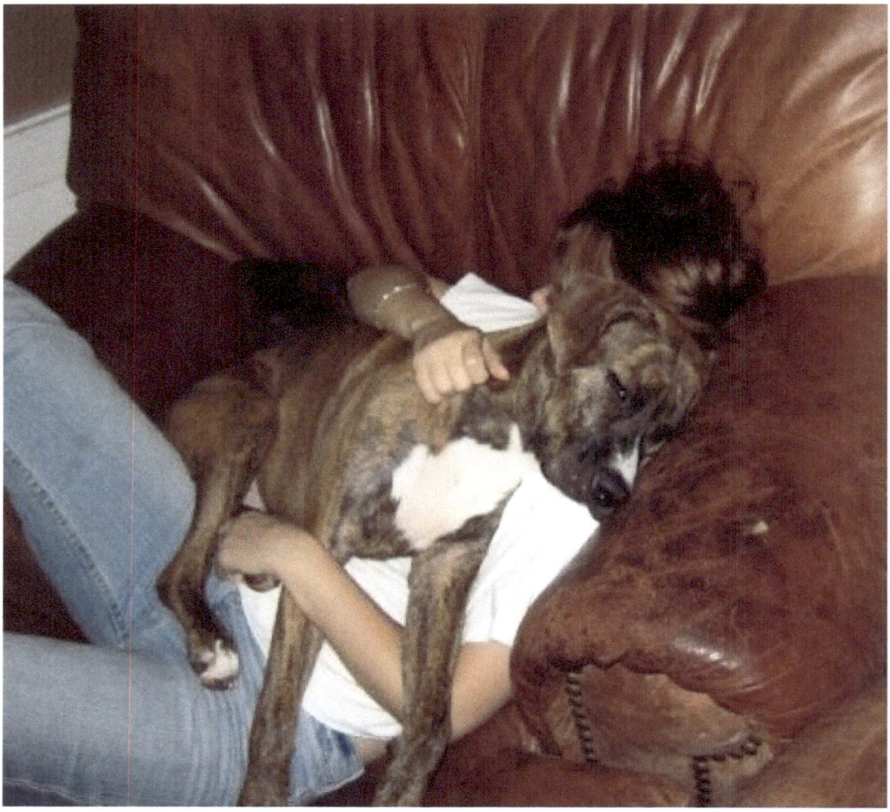

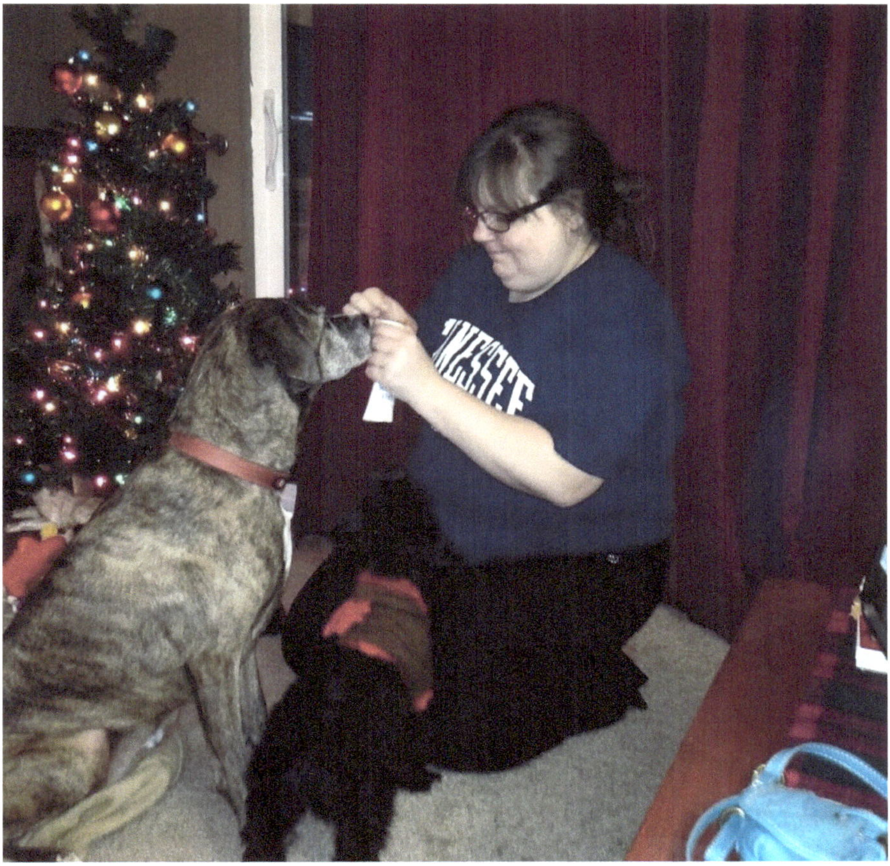

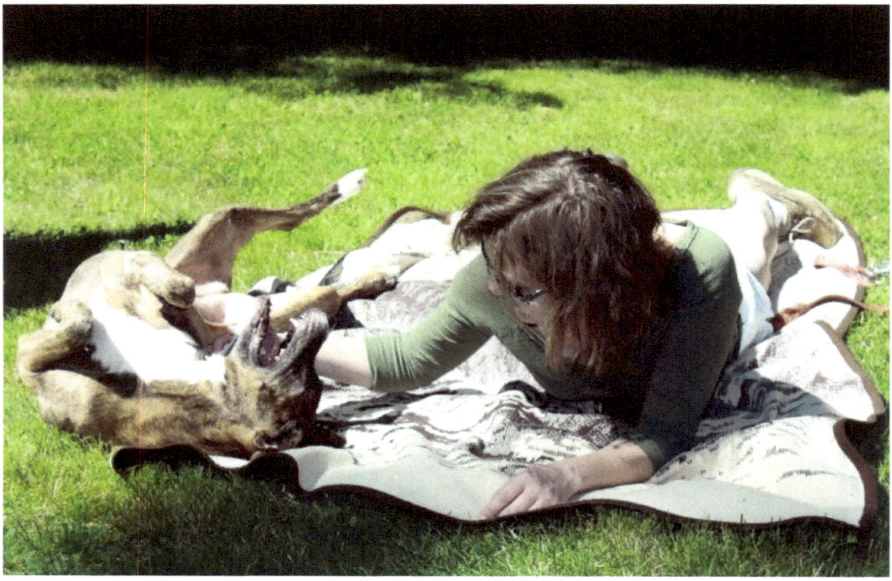

www.ingramcontent.com/pod-product-compliance
Lightning Source LLC
Chambersburg PA
CBHW040347220526
45473CB00009B/2806
* 9 7 8 1 7 1 9 5 7 0 7 2 5 *